# White Bird: A Sequence

&

*Wendell Hawken*

FUTURECYCLE PRESS

*www.futurecycle.org*

Library of Congress Control Number: 2017944798

Published by FutureCycle Press
Athens, Georgia, USA

ISBN 978-1-942371-35-9

*To the caregivers*

# Contents

## 3.

## 4.

## Question

When the white bird comes,
when the secret of wheat
uncovers itself and a terrible
beauty takes up with time
to dance past the glass house
damaged by stone, the owl will
fill the bare fields of night
with her question, always
her question. What else can she ask,
can be asked of herself
and of you who hear through
the maze of your ear nestled
flat on the side of your head,
thin as a shit-eater's grin,
the leer of its learning
the secret of wheat, the kernels of truth
from the seeds of her head—
where else are the dead
to be sprouted?

1.

## Autumn Scene at Evening Stables

Let's say, six o'clock in mid-October
down at evening stables, quilted Carhartt's on.
The hills roll pink with color borrowed from tomorrow.
White's in every word I mumble to the dogs.
Our neighbor's barn a line of yellow squares
as ours must shine for her. She's younger than I am,
has yet to get her horses up.

I've herringboned the stone-dust aisle.
Each halter on its hook, water buckets full,
rakes and pitchforks put away, I've had my whiff
of summer in open bales of timothy, alfalfa hay.
Our horses have the look they get—thoughtful,
far away—chewing grain. Oh, sure, I think about Tahiti,
living life one wall away from other lives. How it is
to take my coffee back to bed and read till nine.
But then I'd have to lock the doors.
Always pee inside. Weed and mow for strangers' eyes.
Lord knows what all.

Halfway up the hill, both dogs turn and wait.
Right on time, I hear his pickup coming down the lane.
The neighbor leads two horses in, as ours stand
deep in appetite. Their slopes of neck and rump,
counter-curving spines gleam under yellow light.
Buckets bang on oak boards. Hooves rustle straw.
I flip the switch and shut the door. Another ordinary day.
Whatever *ordinary* means.

## Ditched

Loose dog, dropped dog,
whatever might be small
and lost and wary,

whatever cannot be caught
with squatted-down soft words,
meaty treats,

sharp-nosed little dog
no longer looking up
at slowing cars for *The Car.*

Dropped dog, loose dog
running back roads
like it knows

where the gravel goes,
like it knows
what it is doing,

who has not been dropped
on unknown rural roads—
gnawed on other creatures'

long-dead bones?
I say, little dog, go in the direction
you least think will save you.

What you fear might protect you.
Come now,
in the breaking open

of this cool clear morning,
that's right,
good dog, come here.

## Diagnosis

A moving apparition
      wanders in,
shadow
      in our front field
         where shadow never is:
stray bull, Picasso-black,
      mammoth horns.
         His black balls
a second disproportion.
      He coughs,
         purple tongue
wagging
      like some horrid stamen,
         lowers his head
on noticing our cows,
      and plows—*he will not scare*—
to where our whole herd, ears out now,
      rises (as if his coming
         is just the thing).
I wave my stick and shout
      but he slips among them, black
         spot in a churning red mass,
to leave me
      standing feet flat,
         broken bough in hand.

## Code I: Husband and Doctor

*What about my sex drive?*
*I've got no interest. None.*

*Your medicines,* says the doctor.
*Any one of them could do it,*
says, *Years*
*since I have seen*
*this kind of patient blow-out,*
*such crashed cells and platelets.*

*A promising new drug that causes*
*limbs to tingle, we'll save for later.*

(Lord knows what he means by
"*tingle.*")

## Code II: Husband and Wife

To my unbuttoning
his shirt's top button,
rubbing his familiar gray-brown fuzz,
he cups his hands around my ass,
pulls me to him, says, *If you want,
I'll try.*

**

Him so quiet in his chair: *What are you thinking?*

*What parts I need to fix the sickle bar.*

**

He eats ice cream now.
Is back to smoking cigarettes.

The front door clicks him going out
to smoke, clicks him coming in.

The smell of smoke is on him
when he asks, *Want to try again?*

## Let Me Be

Let me be your Dusseldorf,

Let me be your Dusseldorf,
your busy wharf, your hard-mouthed horse

or I won't be
your dam that bursts.
Honey, let me be your Dusseldorf.

Let me be your no-bake cake,
your tofu steak, your coffee break.

Let me be
your pesky fly, your me oh my
French apple pie

or I won't be your center aisle,
your wharf at all.

Honey, let me be your juicy steak.

Let me be your Raisin Bran,
your Kubla Khan,
carry water for your Gunga Din,

and I will be your Rin Tin Tin,
your thick or thin,
your double chin.

If you let me be your crocodile,
your hypostyle,
your country mile if you could just stay awhile,

honey, I will catch your stumble,
be your bumble,
patch your crumble.

If you let me be your golden rule,
your three-legged stool, your Liverpool,

you can be my toothless smile,
my sun-soaked isle,
the twister of my Mouse-ka-dial.

If you let me be your work-stained shirt,
your liverwurst, your trip and lurch,

you will be my Demerol,
my woozy squirrel, my cat's hairball,
my wherewithal, my caterwaul,

my continual, consensual, sweet edible,
fat bellyful, my oh so beddable,
incredible adverbial,
non-political,

my celestial, irresistible,
mercurial,
industrial,
my polynomial.

Honey, let me be your downright fool.

## Baseball Cap

His billed cap rests on the counter
where he flung it upside down, waiting
like a ladle
                    no, more a dipper
Big or Little
constellations I can find,

one pouring content into the other
joined together

and sometimes a red Mars
or low-lying Venus: war and love
up there in the stars.

# Tongue

Tongue of fire, bell's intoning,
sex exploding, tongue of wagon
pulling, tongue of belt unbuckling
to whip the child.
Say *Ahhh*.
Hounds in full cry *give tongue*.
Crow tongue split for talk.
Gurkhas excise pack mule tongues.
Beef tongue in the deli case
bigger than you'd think. Thin-sliced,
piled-high mother tongue
on a seeded roll. Forked and tattle,
drawn to sore spots,
wicked fictions tingling salt-sided
wrap a young tongue's
sweet-tipped fibs insisted into fact.
For years, practicing,
the tongue *cleaved* to the roof
of the mouth in case the threat
turned true.
Ongoing *oops* to the mother tongue
one's own mother might have
tasted as a child, jostling
siblings for the first dose
of cod liver oil and whose turn
to lick the spoon. Lamb tongue
bleating for its ewe.

# On Hearing His Childhood Stories

I was never locked in any closet. Afternoons, the ice cream man
stopped his truck beside my childhood house. No one shot my first

dog in plain sight, but even so, nothing's deader than a chicken:
this morning's X-ed eyes of two uneaten hens, piecemeal in the cattle pens—

foxes' night work for the flapping fun. Out here a twin-faun morning
can snap its fingers—just that fast—to dead-calf afternoon.

Prescribing the *promising new drug* his cancer doctor said he would *save
    for later,*
how can later be this soon, when he seems so much himself?

The old cow, on the other hand, off to herself, buzzards circling her eye's
putrid ooze (the odor of my mother's neck when she would say, *Just shoot me.*)

I can tell you where I am when the rifle shot sounds, where I listen
for the second bang until it does not happen,

the killed cow's emaciated carcass winched into the truck (to haul her to
    the kennels
to feed her to the hounds) while at our roadside mailbox—it never stops—

a young fox lies in road-kill gallop, black lips drawn back from interlocking
small white teeth. I was never locked in any closet.

The Good Humor man, as you know, stopped his truck beside my house.
The year our chicks outlived their Easter basket green and blue

and grew to pullets, I saw the yard man lift them, first mine, then my
    brother's,
clasp their flappings close and, like twisting bottle tops, turn their necks
    to *snap.*

I was told that he would eat them. My guess is that he ate them. I thought
    of how
he ate them, though never asked him if he did.

## The Toilet Seat Is Up

Blankets thrown back
mark his place:
a novel's dog-eared page.

There is a heavy-handed
freight train engineer
shrieking through the dark,

then susurrus
with back-beat rumbling,
then winter quiet once again.
The TV room glows blue,

front fields gray with cold
under the low-lying wolf moon
some days away from round.
The toilet seat is down.

## Having Let the Dogs Out to Pee

The last night of the year
or the coming one's first morning,
we stood—his familiar, though shrunken,
shoulder warming mine—listening
to not-too-distant wild cries as our dogs
squatted, ignored the clamor—and what a clamor
between low clouds and snow: high-pitched
yips and chattering intensified
by dark, by us not one hundred percent
cold sober: coyotes—hard to know—maybe three,
or more, now howling back and forth,
moving southward toward the highway
making their neck-hair music,
music to sober up to, to pace the house to,
a get-a-move-on, terrible music
if you are a yearling deer, music to chase away
one shitty year.

## Do Not Resuscitate

*No chest compression?*
Or maybe it was not a *No,*
but a *Not even.*
*Not even chest compression?*

The question she put to me
over half-glasses with what I took to be
incredulity

though less abstract, I admit,
him flat on the gurney
gasping his chest's burning.

## Sick Calf Correlative

Birth defect is the vet's guess. Neurological, his bumping
into trees when his legs so move him. The look of having
passed the portal in his droop-ear flounder, rolled-back eyes,
his underside's spreading impudence of flies,
I would pull him off the clay bog onto a grassy flat to die
but, no, he wants to try; so, twice a day, I dredge
medicated bottles the calf will swallow but not suck,
his lying flat-out, churning bare spots in wheat straw
running sideways in the stall to which we hauled him.
I freshen bedding, hot water bottles. Prop him up as best I can
against pneumonia. The one time he does sit up makes his return
to churning worse, of course. Five days until his breathing stops,
head and neck relaxed in straw. How disbelieving I had been
when my father said, *The hardest thing a body ever does is die.*

2.

## Seeking the Second Opinion

As Saint Bede saw a human life as a small bird
flying from the dark across a lit hall
and out into the dark again,
                                        a cardinal hurls
his red self, flapping at the feed-room window: thump
and drop, thump and drop
                                        stirring equine medicines
along the feed-bin shelf. All he knows: try to fly,
not yet so exhausted as to let
my hands around him,
                                not yet having brought
the barn cats down the loft stairs.

His fear of me sends him higher,
harder at the glass,
                            the feed sack I pick up
too stiff to drape him quiet, though stiff enough
to nudge him toward the lesser light
of the open feed-room door
                                    where his wings recover
weight and measure, flutter righting into flight
out and down the barn aisle to disappear
on the soft air of before.

## Farm Pond Reflection

Weather stayed up late, so late
morning lingers instead in the neighbor's pine bough bed.

Thin fog lies across the front fields, gathering in hollows
vague and pooled as memory gets to be
with its few deep spots.

Wisps of dreams rising from the pond, forgotten
as the hour warms reflective,

hunger closes its coyote eye at the rising
red-tail's cry: *scree, scree.*

Wet-weather ponds again hold ducks and geese.
Thoughts slide like water on a wire
drip-dripping into gravity.

The coffee's good this morning.

Cowbirds score our four-board fence: high notes
erased by squawking flight.

*Oblique, oblique,* chirps a syrinx
well within the cedar in a lower octave's lyric.

Pairs of King birds flutter at each other,
overburdened by desire
though the month seems late for mating.

A sweet dream rises of a younger self, starting in again,
feather pillow folded, a time when *ever after*

stood for good, and he and I believed in lyrics,
believed enough to sing along.

# Gratitude

Every bucket has its horse
beside it down the fencerow.

All three heifers nod up from pasture
coming to their common trough.

Barn cats slink in to be fed: the black,
the brindle: no name other than the color.

Easy to miss this unmarked place,
its drive-past pastures, limestone outcrops,

dried-up farm pond
on a back road shortcut to the dump.

But dark enough to see stars.
Still enough most dawns to hear holly leaves

click their slight percussive
as if welcoming another soft gauze morning.

## *Scree, Scree:* The High Sharp Fighting Cry

A red-tailed hawk—the smaller male, I think—
swoops down to bounce a feet-first landing,

head swiveling, its eyes just-try-me yellow
(like his can be, though pale blue),

shifts once, twice in uncut grasses,
doing the not-dancing slow dance couples do,

then flaps an uplift, grasping a half-grown rabbit,
its haunches with some small gallop left

as if running for its life across the sky,
seeming to assist the hawk's labored rise.

Have you ever heard a rabbit scream?

## Observations after Working the Food Pantry

Hunger takes a number, waits in line
leaning up against an outside wall.

Lines get longer over time.

Hunger can come well-dressed,
drive a good car,
be lost-job hard times.

Sometimes first time hunger cries.

Other hunger has to sit,
points its cane at choosings
off the free-shop shelves.

Hunger might leave an engine
running—for fear it won't re-start.
Keep kids strapped in the car
or let them run around.

Some hunger walks the uphill half mile.

Another hunger cannot bring
itself to come.
And still another hunger is not hungry
though full of appetite.

## Corn Planting Day

All praise this day, the day before
Last-Frost Night when locust trees drip
white with bloom, profuse
but fleeting.

All glory too to Early Girls
ready to get down and dirty.

Praise transfusion's packed red cells,
his grease-stained jeans again

and multiplying
tractor parts across the yard.

For his red count rise: Hallelujah.

Praise IVs of Zometa, hardener of bone,
rows of spinach coming in,
the wild turkey's Jurassic strut:
praise my glancing up in time to see.

A hymn too to Forest Pharmaceutical,
its Lexapro each night for him
and, for me, glory be to Ambien.

## Drive-In Theater

It helps, this thinking metaphorically.
Five orange La-Z-Boys, for instance,
each with a companion seat,
plate-glass window where the screen would go,
the hall's to-and-fro of white-coat actors gawking back
while hooked-up refreshments drip-drip in.

*Zometa, Alkeran,* and every Thursday *Dexamethasone.*
I hear there is an Athens taxi fleet called Metaphor—
imagine scores of Metaphors
speeding tourists here and there, anywhere
but this companion chair
while the chemical to harden bones—*Zometa*—
drip-drips in.
              How hard is too hard?
*Is everyone always this nice?*
He nods, *We're all in the same bucket.*
And I, ever the corrector, especially of him:
*You mean "boat"*
when, no, he was thinking *"bucket."*

## The Meat-Eater's Wife

The meat-eater's wife
knows sinew and bone,
gristle and skin, loosening
joints of hock, leg and thigh,
the opacity of the flounder eye.
Eyes, always the eyes
and a creature's feet
to be overcome
in the turn to meat,
feathers gathered on the fingers
gummed in blood:
blood and feathers joined together.
The meat-eater's wife
sharpens her knife,
a gift at her marriage, the one
before this one, French steel on stone,
to a meat-eater too.
*Chirr chirr* brightens the blade.
The meat-eater's wife
sees the steel smile.
After a while, out comes the board,
its catch-pool for blood,
blood under her nails, carving
flesh to the cravings,
the meat-eater's wife
wielding her knife,
dividing forever
flesh from flesh (*true god*
*from true god*
comes the Sunday refrain:
coupled cars on a train)

the meat-eater's wife
whacking her cleaver,
now and forever,
rhymes with believer,
as the meat-eater's wife
washes and washes her hands.

## In the Know

Ratcheting squirrels on fence boards,
tiny yellow butterflies back from whatever
form in which they wintered,

who knows what knowledge does—
treatment days counting red and white
platelets, charting protein spikes.

He knows current downtown detours,
that Deanna never rolls a vein.

I know to bring a thermos, which snack machine
holds what. For transfusion, to pack lunch.

As forager, I can run the corridors
as well as any laboratory rat.

We both can work the side-tray tables
on the upstairs treatment chairs.

Are not startled when strangers ask
what we might like from Subway
brought back. Or the smiles and waves
as they depart. We do it too.
Or that Deanna hugs us both good-bye—
first him, then me.

Yesterday he taught me what plugs where
to work the power sprayer,
bagworms in the blue spruce
having sucked the top branches bare.

## Ix-nay

The transplant team says *No*.
No *launching pad* (his doctor's image),
no *rolling dice* (again, his doctor).
No forevermore in center city Baltimore.
The transplant team says *No.* No
new marrow
for his good dog bones,
his osso buco, ham steak, ringbone,
suck the marrow full of sorrow,
break the bad news on the phone:
no new tricks for old dog bones.
None to pick. Make no bones.
Tickling no funny bones.
No bare-bone instruments for the end man
in the minstrel show. No deboning
roasts served on china of burnt bone.
Cut to the bone:
the transplant team says *nyet,*
says *nee,* says *ha,* says *la.*
There is no *no* in Irish.
No boning for the test
not given.
No bones to pick, contend with,
turn to music by the end man.
No dice, no funny, lazy, bony stick of macaroni.
The transplant team says *ix-nay,*
*nabo, nein.*
Says *jani, gatu, yox, chikimba,*
*nani, saa, segar.*
In Mongolian, says *bish,*
meaning "not this."

3.

# Repeat

Prayers repeat week on week
beginning the belief

in ritual if not
in resurrection,

bare fruit trees red-tipped budding,
peas a two-leaf promise

needing thinning,
life grows into its meaning

but tell me, will you,
disperse into a universal stew,

and am I therefore here
and now what will be

left of you—like the light left on
I thought was morning

tucked up beneath a quilt
called *Crazy?*

## Voices

Hay barracks stacked with round bales
hauled in from the fescue fields.

*There are periods of stability,* said the doctor.
*You've been lucky, done better than I thought.*

Cloven hooves attached to bone
begin appearing in the yard
while winter holds one hand behind its back.

Dogs reek again of scavenge.
Remaining birds are small and brown
not much song
but some.

*Very lucky.*

At first, I did not mind
hawks' fighting cries: *scree, scree.*

*It feels like a dream.*

*What part?*

*All of it.*

Hospice brings a "Comfort Kit" boxed in cardboard:
morphine's blue to be squirted under the tongue
the way we aced the horses.
Lorazepam. Suppositories. Something
for the end-of-life gurgle
of what they called *actively dying.*

*Just put it in the fridge and forget it.*

I almost do.

Suck and huff of oxygen machine, the new white noise
now louder than the risen peepers.
Ritalin for energy. Also dexamethasone.
Weekly measurements, seamstress-like, of upper arm,
thigh above the knee.
                      Ah, but if you had seen
him in his riding boots and breeches
walking to the barn, his hayfield shoulders.

*From now on, you can't believe anything I say.*

Brambled green underskirts the trees,
soon will express itself in unfurled leaves.

*I'm in purgatory now.*

Soft as night wears off,
the flap of lifting wings: small birds rise.

*Scree, scree.*

*I can't fix things anymore. So much going wrong, it must be me.*

Wasps have taken to the wren house
hanging from the porch eave
visible from the bed set up in the library.

*Not what you'd expect but beautiful to me: a farm gate hanging from a white oak.*
*No one invited me in but I am on an ATV, driving around, horses dodging*
    *as I go.*
*Everyone smiling at me, waving.*

The wasp house on a wire sways
with any huff of air, swaying against the flat blue
like a rowboat on an ocean.

*There is no difference between my dreams and lying right here.*

Birds I can remember seeing
disappear like thoughts into leafy trees,
birds I know I saw
but cannot say what birds they were.
Birds is all.

He is sleeping off his night pain.

Wasps will occupy a birdhouse.
The locust tree leans a little more each spring,
day by day deeper in.

*God wants me to help. He can't be everywhere at once.*

The pillbox's popped tops tell the day and time:
seven days, four boxes each.
start in again at Sunday.

*I don't trust me either. I'm in purgatory now.*

A small wood-colored bird perched on a rocker's back,
eye to eye with me through the panes.
Whatever bird it was, beak open,
staying open as its body pulsed
the same long song three times,
singing for itself, its mate.

*Scree, scree.*

They had said how it would be but did not tell it all,
had shown the scan that showed
blood's dark Rorschach: *And painful.*

*Very painful.*

His oncologist, in the beginning: *I will keep you alive
until something else gets you.*

Tenuous as a wren house on a wire,
a wren house with a wasp's nest in it.

Two drips went in his belly, their attachments
shaped like bottle caps: morphine, of course,
and a tranquilizer, both on long cords
so the drips did not rip out
when he slipped from bed
and the rescue squad put him back.

*Professional,* he murmured, when raised
the first time.

After all the kids, both his and mine, had left: *Are we done?*

He did not gurgle,
his feet two peaks beneath the cotton blanket.

Hands curled at this chest,
gone was pain's quotation mark
between the dashes of his brows.

No gurgle.

*Scree, scree.*

## Like Fear Is Afraid of Itself

Like the tongue is afraid of the teeth,
like the mouth is afraid of the mind,
in the land of the Cyclops, envy the blind.

Like the belly will crave baked bread,
like the hand is drawn to the jaw,
in the hour of twilight, envy the thaw.

Envy the envious brother of Esau.
Envy the tree its stand for the saw.
In the moment of dying, envy the dead.

# Maybe Wolves, Maybe Coyotes

Out walking on familiar farmland, not ours
but land ridden over enough to know,
I am in a dry creek bed.
A calf or lamb wanders down the hill
bleating as a calf bleats
but small and strangely striped.

I am both in the scene
and watching from above.

My elevated self sees
maybe wolves, maybe coyotes, moving
across the ridge, sees my active self
shush the lamb-calf,
scoop it up (what field creature
lets itself be lifted?), sees
the pack notice us and change
direction, not hunting hard but loping
to where we find ourselves beside
an abandoned house.

All first person now, no more
elevated observation,
I rush up shaky wood planks,
pull up two sharp instruments, like knives
but not, embedded in the floor,
gallop up another half flight.

The wolves—they are wolves
by now—will hesitate, I know, at stairs
but still I have to hurry.
I bolt the bedroom door.
There is a long thin lumpy cot
covered in red leather. There is no water.
I wake to lack of water,
the dog beside me in the bed.

## Some Days After

Across the asphalt lot
a smaller brick building
like his workshop with its roll-up door
but brick.
                    Inside on a gurney, a box
resembling one for long-stemmed roses
though oversized, of course. HEAD hand-written
on its top, surname on the side.

*Would you like to see him?*

I came to see him, having heard stories
of cement instead.
                    It's him, alright,
his "1938 Model" purple cap, brim angled
for a nap. Our sheets still wrapped around him.
They have not fiddled with him.

One last quick touch enough,
the burn of cold cannot be taken back
any more than fire,
                    his color pinker
than his darkening at home
as Hospice and the others
did their doings.
                    So maybe a little fiddling.
Unlatching the furnace door,
a roar explodes,
high orange flames deep inside.
His paper box (wooden bottom for support) rolls
onto the metal slab inside.
The door re-latched and that was that,
no taking back as the undertaker,
his young helper, and I left the furnace to its work.

# A Bank Barn's Open Loft Doors

The big, bay thoroughbred, well-mannered,
kind, stands quiet as I strip his wool cooler off.

I turn him to face the huge bank barn,
as big as any I have ever seen, even Amish.

I back him up a slight rise. Never having
sailed a horse, I do not know how

but a friend, whose wife has died, coaches me
from where he stands up in the open loft door.

I undo his leather halter, let it drop into my hand,
step back to watch.

All on his own—no wings or any sail
that I can see—that nice horse lifts off, tucking up

his front legs like a first-rate open jumper
to, sure enough, sail off into the dark loft's open doors.

# Ceremony

I weighed and tasted
his ten pounds
of tasteless gray ash
and grit—surprising, such grit—
flecked with bone.
The kids came after work,
even his son.

Flinging the ash, each cast
arcing a quiet thought
as the larger, whiter bits
dropped closer in,
swallowed up in autumn grasses
as flames will swallow.

Down the lane
to empty cattle pens,
hay barracks, up the hay field
to machine shed, horse barn, workshop,
telling stories as we flung
to finish at his front porch chair
where his kids sat clustered,
dinner plates on laps, talking of the times
he and their mother lived together
some forty years before.

4.

## In the Crevice in the Cedar

Carolina wrens
bring moss and twig,
feed-sack string;
light of early sun
outlines them white,
turns their working wings
translucent
as if bringing light
and maybe luck
by strand of straw,
by piece of twine.

## A Quarter a Prayer

Coins in slots,
color rolls down random,
round as gumball hope,
its weighted shape.
Cup your hand and catch.
Taste the sweet
blown to bursting pink.
All color
chews to pink
and tastes the same:
sweet at first,
then not. Just chew.

## Rhymes with Rain

The song and dance of boiling water, its hot breath
the color of cold

rain on a metal roof,
percussive gurgle down the drains,

rain like paper rustling, a reading rain,
Sunday rain, rain to call your sister rain,

needed rain for seedlings,
bill paying rain,

no need to shut the windows
straight-down nameless rain,

cloudburst rain to stain
the secret velvet of the self

in ceremonies taught on rainy afternoons
to swallowing drains

almost back where one began
but on a softer plane.

There are times I move through darkness
and times darkness moves through me.

The centrifuge keeps to itself,
warp and speed all it needs;

the greater the speed, the greater
the self inside.

The pillow understands the head,
fewer feathers every year.

Letting warmth go
brings a second blanket to the bed.

## Which

Do you ever dream you're sleeping,
dreaming in your sleep,
and the dream inside your dream
is sweet—in the dream you dream
you're dreaming your body in complete
agreement with your bed,
no orphan in your own skin
abandoned on the doorstep of your life.

Sirens of some distant burning,
night sits up and lies back down. The curled cat
fills the narrow of your waist with warming.
Snow melt out there banging down the spouts:
another short gray day struggling to light
according to the cock's recurring call.

Do you ever wish for some one word
to cause your neck to lift, eyes to shut,
and all day say—as my neighbor's rooster
continues to proclaim the coming
of a day half gone—
or would you rather be the cat?

# Autumn in Hunt Country

Tree-frog static. A fox squall.
Crows, of course,
though fewer since the West Nile.

The vivisection dream again.
Another fox squall.

Dew enough
to drip from downspouts.
Foxhound toenails clack on wood floors.

There would be scent this morning.

Retreating mist streaks pastures
white on yellow.

Crab grasses going through
their spreading motions
become an easy pull.

## The Random I Am

The flat black wall of woods
disintegrates
to scrub of bush and vine-clogged tree.

Yellow hunger
closes its night eye.
Sparrows fill their fat throats with song

as I sit out on our front stoop
imagining myself
in the thick of it all,

a shawl of warm sun,
the throat of morning
humming vacant at its center,

laundry flapping on the line:
prayer flags for a future
wafting fresh air, needing to be

taken down.
The perfect cup of last year's fallen
nest, silver-dollar-sized:

woven threads of horsehair
from the red dun quarter horse
and Appaloosa pony.

His illness was the center of a circle
walked around
as the Slavic horse was walked

to death for sweeter meat.
Winter's bare necessities,
the sun less low-slung,

who eats their resolutions
one by one? Sitting on the stoop
in a shawl of warm sun

idly smoothing a clay pot's soil
brings on
an ant explosion:

small brown ant defenders
zig-zag the rim
looking for the random I am

while nurse ants carry huge white larvae
big as they are
to converge and disappear

underground, one by one,
in a kind of nurse-ant order
known only to them.

## On Hearing Crows Discover Turkey Bones
## I Left Out on a Rock

If the raven's right,
if there is no evermore, never
mind. If here and now,
right here at this walnut table
looking out through dog-smudged glass
on a tan grass winter afternoon
warm as early spring, I am, of course,
sitting in my thinning skin-boat
drifting in my downstream,
as he did his, never mind the raven.
Let's go out and listen to those crows
calling kin to turkey carcass, bones and skin
tossed up on a rock after simmer into stock
and soup, the self-same rock as other holidays,
the flat rock beside the paddock
with the old blind pony
whinnying when called, easing
her arthritic joints down paths
she herself created
until the day she doesn't—
that's not today. Today why not
listen to those crows
here and now bringing kin in,
black wings lifting light
risen white with every stroke
(even if the raven's right).

## Harvest Party at the End of the Road

Strung up
across framed 2×4s
high as a house,
higher than the dwelling
(that began as a garage)
up there on a tacked-together
scaffold filling the small yard
hang maybe eighty pelts, mostly red fox,
skinned and flayed, three rows full,
headless, of course, their fur outlandishly
bright against an overcast winter morning.
Six bigger, gray-brown coyote skins center the top row.

People, holding red plastic cups,
mill around. Cell phones click. One guy
sets up a tripod: pelts as party decoration.
Could the three smaller pale orange ones be the kits
raised up between the round bales
stacked in our hay barracks?
Months now since daily sightings.
So tame, they were,
ignoring tractors, not pausing play
to watch us drive by.
Too tame, we feared.

And here I took him soup
when his house burned down,
paid for vegetables at his self-serve stand,
paid what the signs said, and took no change.

## Farm Auction

*Sell everything,* he had said. Sell the batwing bushhog,
rototiller, snow blower, York rake, grapple. *Sell it all.*

Sell the New Holland tractor not yet paid off
together with its front-end loader.

Sell the backhoe used just once to bury our old hound
up beside the horses in the field he thought might

grow alfalfa. Sell the blue-bellied Ford I drove to rake
orchard grass into cut and dried windrows,

him following, his baler spouting round bales.
Sell that hateful baler, always breaking belts.

Good or bad, regardless, sell it all. Hay spikes too.
Sell the creep feeder with three stanchions:

no calves to nurse, unless a neighbor
might bring an orphan or weak twin.

I have that knack, held some nippled bottles back.
But sell the feed troughs, pipe gates, water buckets,

what English saddles the kids don't want.
Western ones can go.

Auction all the leather bridles,
long-shanked bits no one uses any more,

lunge ropes, lead ropes, breast plates, figure eights,
standing martingales—Yep, he liked his horses keen.

*No use riding deadheads you gotta kick along.*
Sell the three-horse slant-load trailer,

the Silverado pickup with its parasitic draw.
Empty out his workshop: lathe, drill press, planer, table saw.

*Sell everything,* the man said, so on the given day
the crows will hear and strut in, full of black and shiny appetite.

Bluebottle flies will stir from diapause. Skunks, of course,
and possums. Vultures drifting ever lower, in tighter circles,

much as water finds a drain
until, box after box, then the machines, all is sold

and hauled off, even the old GMC dump truck
someone figured out how to start.

## Trek to Evening Stables

In the days before another year,
snow of a thousand words
covers the country,
smooths all forms to one: words
you never think
not to know
until all is soft white wordless
and blue lines,
until being
outside is to be
covered by a falling
language other than your own,
words to lighten shaded hollows
shushing the silence
of the little sounds
to a quiet, empty at its center,
time struck by the tongue
anywhere in thickening snow.
Birds perch fluffed
into themselves.
Burrows fill, warm-bodied.
Forage curls suspended
for a time under
all the words for white,
blurring the slow-going
stagger through its deepening
to feed the stabled horses
nickering, striking hooves
at hearing a step they know.
Outside, glancing back
past the filling tracks, how warm
yellow windows seem,

the flicker of firelight,
constancy of table lamps
where a book turned
open on itself lies
ready.

## A Little Lost

It is a blue-gray morning, bluer now.
Bluer in a bright way.

The old dog eases down, negotiating
bones and joints to lie flat out,

then sigh.
Her eyes now follow *me* around.

Pills twice a day, Tramadol and Gabapentin,
the same.

4 a.m., thinking of the breakfast I will not fix:
oatmeal drenched in half & half. Or two fried eggs.

Or the French toast he called *Jersey eggs,*
the French call *le pain perdu.*

The click and drip of time and water.
The neighbor says, *You seem a little lost.*

Bones put out on the rock:
though I know there's possum, crow,

it is the fox I say I feed.
I glimpsed him just this morning

loping off, high-headed, rabbit haunch
sticking out his mouth,

ears swiveled to hear my moving
up the farm lane, not cross-country after him.

## Having Settled on Itself, Quiet Shuts Its Eyes

After all that's said is done:
plates stacked back, scraps set out,
way out, for night appetite I call fox,
after all that's done is said,
X-ed lines signed and dated,
most notes mailed,
quiet curls its tail around the house,
the real cat having dragged back
her day's gray harvest—with any luck
already dead. By quiet, I mean
peepers calling from the pond,
the old dog stretched out wheezing,
the neighbor's roosters.
Same as always, only more so.

# Acknowledgments

Grateful acknowledgment is made to the following publications, in which these poems appeared, some in earlier versions.

*Shenandoah:* "Tongue"
*Poet Lore:* "Autumn Scene at Evening Stables"

These 18 poems, some in a slightly different form, appeared in *Fish Anthology 2015* (Fish Publishing, Cork, Ireland), as part of the winning Short Memoir manuscript, titled *Throat of Morning:* "Diagnosis," "Let Me Be," "The Toilet Seat Is Up," "Do Not Resuscitate," "Trek to Evening Stables," "*Scree, Scree:* The High Sharp Fighting Cry," "Corn Planting Day," "Gratitude," "Farm Pond Reflection," "In the Crevice in the Cedar," "Observations after Working the Food Pantry," "The Meat-Eater's Wife," "Repeat," "Ix-nay," "The Random I Am," "Autumn in Hunt Country," "Harvest Party at the End of the Road," "Some Days After."

With thanks to Marie Pavlicek-Wehrli, Bob Ayers, Mary-Sherman Willis and Kara Olson for their help with this manuscript. To Susan Sindall for her years of help with my craft. To the entire Warren Wilson MFA family of writers. And to Vaughn, whose courage runs through this collection.

*Cover artwork, "Great Egret,* Ardea alba*" by Brocken Inaglory; author photo by Daphne Dunning; cover and interior book design by Diane Kistner; Adobe Garamond text with ITC Highlander titling*

## About FutureCycle Press

FutureCycle Press is dedicated to publishing lasting English-language poetry books, chapbooks, and anthologies in both print-on-demand and Kindle ebook formats. Founded in 2007 by long-time independent editor/publishers and partners Diane Kistner and Robert S. King, the press incorporated as a nonprofit in 2012. A number of our editors are distinguished poets and writers in their own right, and we have been actively involved in the small press movement going back to the early seventies.

The FutureCycle Poetry Book Prize and honorarium is awarded annually for the best full-length volume of poetry we publish in a calendar year. Introduced in 2013, our Good Works projects are anthologies devoted to issues of universal significance, with all proceeds donated to a related worthy cause. Our Selected Poems series highlights contemporary poets with a substantial body of work to their credit; with this series we strive to resurrect work that has had limited distribution and is now out of print.

We are dedicated to giving all of the authors we publish the care their work deserves, making our catalog of titles the most diverse and distinguished it can be, and paying forward any earnings to fund more great books.

We've learned a few things about independent publishing over the years. We've also evolved a unique, resilient publishing model that allows us to focus mainly on vetting and preserving for posterity poetry collections of exceptional quality without becoming overwhelmed with bookkeeping and mailing, fundraising activities, or taxing editorial and production "bubbles." To find out more about what we are doing, come see us at www.futurecycle.org.

## The FutureCycle Poetry Book Prize

All full-length volumes of poetry published by FutureCycle Press in a given calendar year are considered for the annual FutureCycle Poetry Book Prize. This allows us to consider each submission on its own merits, outside of the context of a contest. Too, the judges see the finished book, which will have benefitted from the beautiful book design and strong editorial gloss we are famous for.

The book ranked the best in judging is announced as the prize-winner in the subsequent year. There is no fixed monetary award; instead, the winning poet receives an honorarium of 20% of the total net royalties from all poetry books and chapbooks the press sold online in the year the winning book was published. The winner is also accorded the honor of being on the panel of judges for the next year's competition; all judges receive copies of all contending books to keep for their personal library.

www.ingramcontent.com/pod-product-compliance
Lightning Source LLC
Chambersburg PA
CBHW070012100426
42741CB00012B/3207